IN A RIVER OF WIND

Poems by Neil Harrison

For Roy,

I hope you enjoy some of these.
It was really good to meet you at
the Norfolk Arts Center. I really enjoyed
your reading there. All the Best,

Neil Harrison   5 October '06

IN A RIVER OF WIND

ISBN 0-9702851-0-8

Cover painting: "Missing Mountains" by Neil Harrison
Back cover photo by the author.

Cover Design, Layout, and Graphics: Eddie Elfers

Thanks to Gretchen Ronnow, Curtis Meyer and Eddie Elfers

Bridge Burner's Publishing Company
PO Box 5255
Mankato, MN 56002-5255 phone: 507-389-1535
www.bridgeburners.com

For Larry Holland
(1937-1999)

With deep respect and that abiding love for words
I first learned in his writing class twenty years ago.

Table of Contents

A River of Wind:

Postscript:

Preface

In Your Dream of Dreams
(for Richard Hugo, 1923-82)

A snow leopard lost in the lowlands
paces at the edge of an inland sea,
bound by instinct into that water
and across to the familiar mountain, home.

In a dream you search for an ancient key
to the darkest room in a house of books
where you once dreamed tracking an answer
to the source, "In the beginning was . . ."

Enveloped now in a necessary cold
the endangered remnant presses on.
You feel it dawning, a travesty of light;
the pulse of the mystery grows dim.

Perfect camouflage in a wrong niche,
stalking to and fro on the earth,
these fallen predators—my God!
You wake, missing mountains.

Walking Alone

Dawn

Warm mornings, mid-March, I leave the cabin
in the dark, and jog the shoulder of the highway
down to the entrance to the state park, bridge
planks clumping over Chadron Creek as I pass
headquarters, the maintenance yard, and follow
the winding blacktop south past vacant corrals,
abandoned cabins, the empty, padlocked swimming
pool on the ridge overlooking the Deadhorse burn,
up through the pines and dirt-specked drifts
to the top of the world in time to face
that old mystery climbing in the east.

Elkhorn

Parts of this river I know
by heart, from those years
with my brother and the years
without, before NO TRESPASSING
became a sign of the times.

Each summer we'd splash
after carp in the shallows,
every fall I'd hunt deer
with a bow, alone, putting
together pieces of the river,

learning these oxbows
west of Broken Bridge, thirty
miles of swamps and nameless lakes,
stagnant remains of the old bed
each time the channel cut a new,

flowing through the seasons
on her secret way, carrying
evidence of each along,
flood waters, sandbars, autumn
leaves and ice, coming, going,

an eternal state of flux.
You can find her name
and image on a million maps,
but she's a mystery a man can only
learn in part, in those places
he's come to know by heart.

Story

A pheasant rose cackling
out of a pocket of cattails.
A boy shouldered his borrowed
twelve-gauge and fired.

His first bird fell
into gold rushes.
He ran to where he thought
it should be, but it wasn't.

He circled, circled
cursing and crying.
At last he found it,
a bright dead jewel.

He carried it back
to the car, to the others.
He held up his kill.
He told them his story.

Neil Harrison

Loading Out Boars

Another Saturday night, Sid backs his long rig up
to the middle chute at the east dock and hands me
the pink release to transport Boardman's boars,
so I set the catch pen and open gates back to the 1800
alley, where the air goes suddenly rank ammonia,
and I can hear them breathing out of sight, coarse
files rasping the planks of the tight enclosures

in the boar alley where there's no lights, and as I
make my way past their separate pens, one barks,
then a volley of WOOF's and they're all up, great-
jowled jaws working overtime, smacking and grinding
in the stinking dark, and something's coming over me,
a wave of meanness, instinct perhaps, rush
of adrenaline, five senses screaming DANGER! DO NOT

ENTER! but instead of flight I'm banging the planks
with an oak cane reinforced with plastic pipe,
yelling like a madman, mindless as these son-of-a-
bitching boars. I open 1813, step out of the way
behind the gate, hammering, hollering, hazing a 700-
pound mass of rage and muscle out the narrow alley
and toward the chutes, then turn another out of 1812

and prod his grunting silhouette out to the main alley
where the first one waits, and with a clatter of hooves
they come together, massive shoulder to shoulder,
shoving and groaning, tossing and roaring, slamming
each other into the steel gates that line the alley,
as I go on turning out boars—1811, 1810, 18-oh-9,
oh-7, oh-6, oh-5, oh-3, oh-2, oh-1, oh-oh—each

exploding into rabid fury, foam flinging from his
churning snout as he skates into the battle royal
I'm aiming for the catch pen, inching up and whamming
a giant Duroc across his inflated foot-long balls

11

(is THIS why we call it pigskin?) then jumping back,
clambering over the nearest fence, flinging alley gates
behind them, shouting, cursing, prodding, laughing

at this oversized package of instant fight
with its loud squeal of a warning label:
A DOZEN BOARS
DO NOT MIX WELL!

Pterodactyls

After sundown on the railroad bridge
I break open the pack of cigars
my brother ripped off that afternoon,
and thank my lucky stars I was there
when he came out the back of Rollie's,
reached down the front of his pants
and pulled them out, grinning 'til he
found them filter-tipped; then scowling,
cursing, Goddamn the luck, he threw
the new pack of Omegas down the alley,
and went back and stole some King Edwards.

So I'm smoking a bona fide pack-a-my-own,
sitting on a pier on the old Black Bridge,
my baitcaster propped across my knees,
the unfiltered stink of Catfish Charlie
rising with the Omega to my lips
each time I puff to keep the bugs away,
when all at once overhead in the dark
something squawks, and my skin shrivels
from the groin on up; a fresh cigar
drops off my lip, pack a' matches slips
out of my hand, and I'm staring up,
ten feet above, at a pair of—Godalmighty!

Giant wingbeats pushing, pulling prehistoric
silhouettes across the sky, long-beaked
necks coiled up like snakes, dark bone
legs thrust back like spears, they sweep
slow-motion over the bridge, out of sight;
I squat, wondering if it's some bad dream,
'til another godless squawk in the dark
and I'm gone, across the bridge to the pier
my brother's fishing. Hey, I call,
and the orange glow of a lit cigar arcs
around to face me. Hey, my brother answers.

13

What's up? he asks. I'm outta' matches.
He gets up slow, hands me his lighter.
How're them filtered sons-a-bitches?
I shake one out, light up and cough,
Huh-hnn-not bad. Bulll-shit, he says,
takes back his lighter. You see them
herons a minute ago? Herons? I echo.
Them two ya' mean? His glowing King Edward
rises and falls. My breath comes easy
all at once. Sure I saw 'em; noisy bastards.
I flick off an ash, saunter back to my pier
and suck on that warm Omega.

October Evenings

I put the arrow back in the quiver
and walk out in moonlight, a ghost
of shadow following like dust
behind a combine, a fine chaff
sifting out of the iron guts of night,

[handwritten: So many Questions — Why an arrow? Whats he doing? Hunting?]

[handwritten: Not anchored in the scene very well]

as the hum of grain dryers takes me
back to the fall of '81, those days
with Carl on the road for Redex, going
north on coffee and credit-card gas,
servicing dryers in Minnesota.

Carl starting units on farms outside
Wadena, me replacing worn-out screens
on a dryer east of Moorhead, the two
of us scraping out caked ash
after an elevator fire near Fergus Falls.

We were working a few miles out of Graceville
when an auger caught my thumb;
I jerked it back, torn and bleeding,
smiled later when the night nurse stitched it,
thankful it was still mine.

It's a song of harvest, October evenings
when you walk out alone in the fading light,
the hum and echo of distant dryers, the rasp
of your breath amid the screaming leaves,
a chorus you don't share with a living soul.

[handwritten: What is a song of harvest? The hum of dryers?]

Those Days

Years ago, when he still had the farm,
seven white sows and a great Duroc boar,
an old Ford tractor and an eighty in corn,
pasture on the creek for a cow and her calf,
thirty-some chickens and a handful of cats,

my uncle had two dogs he called Happy
and Lucky, named I guess for what he felt
at the time; I felt it too, watching him
milk his cow, feed his hogs, plant his field,
pat his dogs, loving those days on the farm

before he lost it, those quiet years before he
started drinking, before the debt came due on
those gilt-edged days that summer afternoon—
one of his dogs had a litter of seven,
Happy or Lucky, and he shot them all.

Flood

He took the fish one June in Wyler's Bend
and walked the half mile home,
his hand in the gill, dragging the blue
to the tree at the north end of town,

where he punched a length of baling wire
through the tough hide behind the bone
rasp of teeth, and hung his catch,
severed the tail and let her bleed.

He sat on an ash stump, lit his pipe
and stared west over his garden, rich
with the soil and stink of a May flood,
until the evening shadows found him,

and with a pair of pliers,
he stripped that yard of flesh,
ran his butcher knife up from the vent
and back between ribs and gills.

He freed the guts, snapped the spine,
left the head a horned ornament in the tree,
and sliced the biggest catfish
the river would give him
into a season's worth of steaks.

A dozen years later they straightened
the river, routed it around the town,
dammed the old channel
and called it flood control,

but each year the crows come
pouring out of the south,
and gather in that dying elm
east of the old man's house,

where a reeking skull on a length of rust

goes on flooding the valley
with the spirit of the river
in the wash of the summer sun.

Journey

Seven kings
rode proud
white stallions;
one man rode a stone.
Seven fell
in a desert hell;
one rides on

alone.

Skulls on the Niobrara

Polished bronze in the shallow water,
bleached white on the bank above,
two skulls on the Niobrara,
bison from another age;
I marked the crossing
on my plastic map.

All afternoon they rattled low
on the floor of my black canoe;
by night my dreams were bison,
skulls crawled across my chest,
whispering years of slaughter
from severed tongues.

Midnight a thunder woke me,
clouds like a dark skin drum
buried a billion brilliant hooves,
rubbed out the white horn moon.

Chanting low in the canyons
a hundred thousand skulls
asked the Running Water—Why?
What god had brought them down?

When the Niobrara raised her voice
the drumming stopped,
my pulse ran black.

At dawn
I erased the map.

Let the river keep her secrets.

In the Beginning

You can see them moving
under the water, schools
of slick-winged miracles,
tails fanning the fine
silt, raising blossoms
of mud in the shallows

in that timeless space
where the world begins
as it always has
in a fecund calm
on the bottom,

and you know
in the instant
for this you were born,
the eternal beginning,
and two worlds waiting
even as it slips away

true to your aim,
the arrow low enough
to counter refraction,
to pierce the illusion
of a peaceful genesis
with the sudden bloom
of blood in the shallows.

The Sandhills Night

Thirteen hours in the field, then dinner,
and out again—slop the hogs, milk the cows,
feed the calves, the summer chores,
and when they're done, walk the hundred yards
out to the road, down the bare sand ruts
in the lane, and turn to face the home

place, different now in the distance,
barn and sheds and four-room shack consumed
in shelterbelt silhouette, an insignificant
blot against the night, and there in the dark
each night you wait, until you can hear it all

again, your father humming in the barn,
forehead pressed into a warm flank;
he's stripping white streams into a metal pail,
aiming at one of the barnyard cats, laughing
at the end of another of the good old days.

You laugh too, eyes overflowing, until reason
takes hold, unravels your father, loose black
strands of wool in the night, and you walk
up the lane toward a warm yellow promise,
a dim but definite square in the dark.

Another Pilgrim's Progress

Sixteen years of Christian morals,
twenty-six battling the bottle and more,
your up-and-downhill pilgrim's progress
from God's sweet saint to the devil's whore
and back again through the hopeless maze
where every path leads to the ledge,
and the choice is fall, for good or evil,
or trust yourself on the razor's edge

where everything depends on balance
and gods and devils hold no sway;
you close your eyes and learn to follow
your Self, the straight and narrow way;
walk blind until your world converges,
all the light and dark things meeting,
then ask your Self to stop, look down—
your feet aren't even bleeding.

Some Autumn

Some autumn as you're passing
through western Wyoming,
an evening with full moon
and blood-red horizon,
blue shadows on sage flats,
foot hills and canyons,
the high plains breathing
gentle ice down your spine,

you'll turn off the highway,
leave your car and say nothing
as you walk into the season
of long nights, the north,
to the place you were dreaming
those nights you woke screaming,
forlorn as the wind
in your wild coyote lungs.

Parnassus

Above Fort Robinson the Pine Ridge ends
suddenly in the badland face of the grasslands,
the Oglala north to the South Dakota border,
the Buffalo Gap beyond.

On the edge of the Ridge,
from the precipice at the top of that world
you can see its end in the ruin below,
a gravel cache of ancient bones
on the floor of an inland sea.

Oracle at the foot of a forgotten mountain,
mother of the muses, house of breath,
electric synapse between words
seamlessly welding the worlds.

Years I've been putting the pieces in place,
committing that view from the Ridge to mind;
tonight, from the summit of this tower of words
I will call her by name and burn.

Weathering
(for Don Welch)

In the gentle seasons
in simple celebration
some begin recording
the weathers of their lives.

But some keep right on scribbling
through the winters, through
the wars; strained, familiar
voices, no one can explain.

Who can explain these starlings
camped on my neighbor's chimney,
why even in the dead of winter
some birds sing.

After the Channeling

Out of the army I waded the Elkhorn
looking for water deep enough to harbor fish,
barely wetting my ankles in holes where
the river had once gone over my head.

I caught stunted catfish in a ghost
of the river my brother and I had known,
more snakes than fish, every bend a refuge
for black whips draped on driftwood, sunning.

The Last Day of October

The furnace kicks on, first time this year,
scent of fuel oil rising with heat in the vents
as I put on coffee, let out the dog,
the sky clear, north wind cold,
sun out of sight behind the garage,
frost on the neighbor's windshield.

Inside, clock ticking, steam curls
off the pot on the stove where I brew
a dream of warmth, a charm against November,
as rich with scent and promise as campfire
on a mountain, as frail as a screen of smoke
against the approaching dark, the cold.

A high-pitched bark, her anxious summons,
and I'm at the door, cup of coffee smoking
like a cauldron in my hand, a small white
lie of warmth on this October morning
where the sky, clear a few minutes ago,
now churns a curled mass of grey,
first storm of the season coming on.

Some Nights

A year-old pup in a cattail slough, he climbs
thin air after a cackling pheasant,
comes down with a mouthful of feathers,
eyes so wild he could fly away with the bird.

Dark as midnight, glistening, he swims again
the long pit, across the icy water and back
against the wind with the crippled teal,
something struggling to get away in his eyes.

And some nights I hunt the field alone,
out to the road where he lies, black
as silence in the ditch, and his eyes
tell me he knows what is stalking us all.

29

This Long Spring
(for Paul)

Odd, the way things come together, thoughts
of Blake, his contraries, scent of lilacs
and new-mown grass on this warm morning,
the 7th of June, at the door to the church
and another season, another dark
wedding of heaven and hell,
farewell to a mental traveler.

Three weeks ago when you asked my plans,
up at the park where we both ran,
I grinned, and told you I'd be fishing,
the carp were moving in to spawn; you were going
back on the road, make the long runs for summer cash.

In the shallow bog above Spring Lakes, big fish
cruising the tepid water, I watch a boy stop,
cock his spear, thrust too high,
into the soft mud. "Aim lower," I tell him,
like my uncle told me before the weight of his years
left him too weak to wade, "they're always
deeper than they seem."

Watching Joe stalk carp with a spear,
it's like seeing myself from a long way off;
I know we'll never grow tired of this,
just too worn out to carry on.

The magnum's effect was immediate; the bullet
separated brain and spine and she fell
as she'd stood, then let it go,
the cold pain of all those years
I couldn't lift her out of.

The grave finished, I walked to the river,
half a mile down from where she once

went through the ice and I went after,
moving out until the thin sheet gave,
then wading waist-deep through the frigid current
to where she was patiently swimming in place;
we shivered together when I carried her out.

I dream of ice and fish and fire—of seventeen years
with a small brown friend; of a boy,
a spear pulsing in his hands;
of fighting sleep on the long haul
through a black night in Montana,
your sudden slip into that false dawn,
truck and trucker going over,
over and over in this long spring
of long good-byes.

A Fog of Clouds

Remembering Sand

Last night on the river,
everything clear, everything
quiet for hours in moonlight,

sand as bright on the bar
downstream as in our camp
below Black Bridge those nights

we built our fires at dusk,
drank beer, fed the flames,
talked on and never noticed

how the moon was changing
everything, until we stood
to relieve ourselves, barefoot

under the stars, and found
the sand strange all at once,
fine, cool, the color of snow.

The Word

Imagine yourself moving
without a word like "walking,"
and imagine seeing,
hearing something
you have no words
to describe.

Say a flock of pheasants
bursts from the brush
beside you, a "you"
without any words
to put your world
together.

No "flock" there, no
"burst," no "brush,"
no colors,
feathers,
cackles,
birds.

No name for the sight,
for the sound,
the something,
no name for anything,
no "you."

How integral these groups of phonemes, magic
as cement, these abstract marks we make
to conjure and in time create
a concrete world out of
the eternal, intangible
wonder of being.

Imagine them, the primordial parents naming
the elements of their dream, of this
dream, each sound, each syllable

filling an image with the breath
of life, giving to a world
the means of life.

In the beginning was . . .

The Gypsy

She arrives in a magic moment;
you turn away, stranger to yourself,

find her ecstatic when you return,
take her with you here and there,

spend seventeen years unaware
of the mystery in this gentle gift —

she's teaching a thing you never knew,
a love that will last you to the end,

and when she's gone, when the lesson's done,
you will know there will be no end.

Faraway Home

Open then
like the hand of a friend
from a faraway home
who promised once to lead you back
through a game you used to play
to the place you could not stay—
the kingdom of words
where all things merge
for the child/creator
of the secret worlds.

Neil Harrison

In My Father's House

Studying the unique archways for the first time
in my father's house, I wonder what made him decide
on them, how he built them in these plaster walls,
and why I never noticed before the various levels
and planes, how this house too holds a separate mansion
for each perspective from which it's seen.

Closing my eyes, I try to picture us then, my two-year-old
brother, mother and me in this basement forty years ago,
my father, creator of noises, above us, walking,
working, building our home. If I listen long enough
in the dark, I can hear it again it seems, that lullaby
of saw and hammer still ringing through my days and dreams.

Perspective

When they dammed the creek in Sherman County
my brother and I rode out to Loup City
one morning with my uncle, and fished all day
while he pushed dirt for the dam.

On the way home that evening, I leaned over
the twelve-pack on the seat between us
and watched my uncle push his '55 Ford
up over a hundred miles per hour.

He was generous with the beers, and I was
only twelve, soon nodding in and out of a long
string of yarns about fat fines and narrow escapes
on the fast track back to Stanton.

God only knows how he hammered those old Fords
to and from jobs in Iowa and Minnesota;
now he rarely drives, never at night, one eye
dim with scar tissue from an old splinter of steel.

I was riding along a couple days ago when he
brought in his mom for her annual checkup;
we were limping along doing thirty-five
when a kid in a Buick blew by us going sixty.

"Christ!" old Bess sat up and growled,
"Where's the fire?!"

Before We Fell

Before we fell to work,
my uncle soaked the burlap jackets
wired around our jugs of water,
put them in the shade
under the dash of his pickup,
and with four five-gallon cans of gas
and a full greasegun in the back,

drove south down the long lane,
west over the white rock road,
turned north onto a sand trail
and we bounced over the sweet
grass of his hayfield in the heart
of the Sandhills,

up to an old Ford
tractor and a dump rake,
where the hay lay
curled in ragged mounds
and meadowlarks stood
greeting us with song.

On the High Plains

Three-year-old pup with more heart
than sense, she dove into buck brush
in a shallow draw on the Pine Ridge;

I waited on the rim, expecting grouse,
but nothing moved below me.
I thought, Snake! and whistled.

Ears down, tail tucked,
she came out of the tangle,
nose, lips and gums full of quills.

Back at camp, shivering by the fire,
she watched me grip the white ends,
one by one, and pull them out.

Crooning to her, cursing porcupines,
I saw her eyes, near-wild at first,
grow calm as the high plains night.

I flicked the last quill
into the dark and stood
to stretch; she shook herself.

We turned our backs to the dying fire;
you could almost touch the nearest stars.

Sunrise on the Verdigris
(for Don Welch)

Numb to the knees in the frigid current
I wade upstream in the pre-dawn mist
through smoking bends in the Verdigris,
the wooded banks dark as scars
bone-deep in the fossiled hills.

Stalking rainbows in a steaming canyon,
I'm twenty yards below an old stick dam
when I see the sun unwrap the sumacs,
color scattered like Christmas ribbons
discarded on the valley floor.

All at once the present opens,
revealing gifts from the past—
a Canada morning, twelve years back,
secret waters, golden trout,
the cry of the loon at dawn.

Something's moving on the ridge
above me, several, white, coming
single-file; another time
I'd simply name them,
let my eyes call them Charolais.

This morning they will be unicorns
down to drink from the copper creek
because at the bottom of this
bovine world, we both know
they are.

Learning the Woods

Cutting firewood along the Platte,
backpacking in northern Wyoming,
I've wished I knew more about trees.

One March at a bookstore
in Lincoln, I find a copy
of THE MASTER TREE FINDER.

That April I'm out at Yellowbanks,
studying scrub oak and sumac
on ridges north of the Elkhorn.

I know this same mix of trees
lines the hills southeast toward Lincoln,
northwest to the Missouri bluffs.

I'm sitting beneath one of the larger oaks,
watching wind on the leaves, when
suddenly I hear a faint whispering.

As I'm nodding off, the great oak
leans closer, opens its wooden pages,
exposes its very essence to me.

I close my eyes on this stroke of luck,
stumbling onto THE MASTER TREE
my first day out with the FINDER.

Neil Harrison

Hunting the Cool of the Day

Quartering into the wind
near the end of the season
we move west through the long grass,
down separate swales along the Platte,
tracking something big in the thicket between us,
convinced we are about to surprise it.

Quiet, in camouflage, we are near enough
I can see you turn when it sounds—
the voice of the lord in his garden;
something like antlers whirling in the brush
clattering low through the branches behind us,
offering not so much as a glimpse at the back parts.

We stare at one another, breathless, shivering,
each hoping it was the other he saw,
though the cover of leaves fell months ago
and even in camouflage we know
we are naked as sin.

Moondancer

When she saw him in June
my sister smiled, shook her head—
Those glass eyes; I don't know.
Her husband nodded—There's something
pretty spooky about a walleyed horse.
I studied those eyes again
and shrugged—Let's just say
they're blue.

Under a full moon one August night
I crossed the pasture, calling him;
he snorted, circled to get my scent,
a quick, stiff dance, and down he came,
proud, white as a muscled ghost,
muzzle down, moving in, and I
fathomed the depths of aqua moons
when I looked into his eyes—
his eyes!

Evensong

Shotgun on this ride, I grab the wing-window post,
another tall-boy Curs, and resume a careful study
of this carefree work of art—
                            Big Al, winding his
brother's Fairlane up a two-rut sand trail north
of Meadow Grove, elbow cocked out the open window,
two fingers playing the wheel,
                           in the Ford I sold
his brother (Thank God!) a week and a half ago, Al
guns over the loose sand, tips his head back, drains
his beer, drops the empty over his shoulder—
                                'Clink'
in the backseat, 'BE-L-L-CH!' up front, then 'tink,'
'tink,' 'POP!' and Al says, "goditsabeautifulnight,"
and I say, "yuhitis," as the car bucks—
                            'WHOOOOM!'
'WHOOOM!' 'WHOOM!' over the high-center trail like
an outlaw mule, then, 'CLUNK!' 'R-RO-O-O-O-AR!'—
his brother's dual exhaust
                        falls,
lost to the Sandhills night, and Al,
the very picture of peace, passes all,
understanding.

The Pigeon Racer
(for Don Welch)

Patient as a man who's waited
forty days and forty nights
in the far-too-pregnant belly
of a three-hundred cubit craft,

he pilots a chair at a backyard table
in a mid-Nebraska college town,
perusing a pigeon-racing journal,
scouting the familiar pages,

eyes going often to the loft,
scanning the sky for a distant speck,
searching the poker-faced clouds
for a sign, some clue
to where he stands in the game.

Fox

Just after dawn on my drive to work,
I see a fox running parallel to the road
and realize if I was younger I'd race him,
then wonder why when he crossed my path,
as I now know he will,
with nothing under heaven
but my car to stop him.

When I let off he goes for it,
rushing mad for the other side,
knotted shoulders and wire-tight back
rolling in sync with those driving thighs,
a single muscle, all red-furred heart,
wild, magnificent, one of the mansions
gracing the house of God.

At Blue Hole

Autumn wind ripped yellow leaves off
cottonwoods surrounding the long pit
where I bent low and he crouched at heel,
stalking the little raft of teal.

They flushed, I shot and two birds fell;
he lunged for the nearest
and brought in the drake as the south wind
carried the hen away from shore.

Out again but not far enough
he turned to me and I signaled,
sorry when he circled and swam on,
too far I thought for a half-grown pup.

Going out was easy, riding the waves,
but when he picked her up and came around
he faced the wind and the long way back,
and I cursed; he seemed to be swimming in place.

Then he was coming, plodding
but gaining, and I was walking out,
something inside pulling, knowing
part of the heart that would bring him in was mine.

When his feet touched bottom and he shook himself
he nearly fell in the shallow water, and his tail
began that timeless dance as he dropped the warm
bluewing in my trembling hand.

Fellow Wayfarer
(for Boris of the Altai Mountains
and for Gretchen)

Looking for a sign in the heavens
I was neither wise nor a man
but stood amazed as my uncle

those evenings in the Sandhills
the stars surreal satellites
white fireflies almost in reach

in a shallow-minded piece of sky
we searched for the frigid war
machine of an imagined enemy

every foreign blinking light
fantastic as our fear of you
and those who christened you

Sputnik we could not comprehend
a name embracing all of us
earthborn fellow travelers.

Autumn

Blackbirds flock the brittle fields
where I lose myself each day at dusk

waiting for something I can't explain
until it happens late one evening

the air, clear and raw as metal
rings like a distant bell

as I search the sky
for particle or wave

and name them both
in a whisper

Geese!
Imagine

what that lead bird feels
drawing her beat by beat

into that nothing
we call the night.

Listen to her
the point of it all

aiming that long noise south
echoing the call she follows

a voice we've lost
the sense to hear.

See them coming? Under the full moon
soundless blue shadows skating the river ice

puzzling out the riddled channels of the Platte
or another of those winding dreams that take them home.

The Picture in My Hand

Leaving the ground again
a lean brown dog is rising
over December bluestem,
held mid-leap forever
in the picture in my hand

Climbing into a clear sky
wide as her boundless
heart, going up once more
farther now and faster
than I can follow

After something higher
than those late-rising ringnecks
she flushed from pockets of tall grass
and climbed after, into the sky

Now in the picture in my mind
held mid-leap forever
over December bluestem
a lean brown dog is rising,
leaving the ground again.

In Your Deep Dream

From a narrow pier
you cast a red spoon
into a school of fish,
gar or pickerel, and
hook something solid,

your rod arcs down,
the end of the pier
begins to sink, you
straddle the boards,
tighten your grip,

consider your knife
and cutting free
as water slowly
climbs your chest,
comes over your chin;

in the end
you hang on,
ride the pier down
into the dark
where the big one
waits.

A River of Wind

Nebraska

When I was a young man and had visions
no one believed me.

Now I am an old man
and dream dreams.

Stalking into the Wind

With a Browning recurve and six cedar arrows
you follow faint shadows, scents and sounds
into thick-woven riparian tangles,
tracking the invisible makers of trails.

Near dusk, stillhunting the water's edge, you hear
the Elkhorn shatter and through a screen of willows
see a whitetail lord cross the golden river,
weird antlers plaited as a crown of thorns.

You are sixteen, learning to merge with the wind,
with the river and the brittle season,
to make your wooden weapons part of you,
and yourself another ghost in the shadows.

Flush!

He is all
cackles and wings
working west under fire,
blotting the sun
and seeming safe
  but seventy yards
  beyond the last shot
  the ringneck begins
  to climb a column of air,
  heart-shot, I know;

I've seen it before.
You watch these birds go up . . . up . . .
forgetting gravity,
clawing toward clouds,
convincing you
they'll never come down . . . then
  something peaks;
  something falls.
  You gather hulls.

Learning Fishing

A Sunday after Bible school
with my uncle up at Gavin's Point
we cursed a string of fishermen
who'd avoided church and got there first,

then lugged our gear to an open spot
in the ragged line where Uncle Dick
cast thirty feet to show me how
and settled back with his bottle to fish.

I heaved out too, six feet or so,
propped my rod on his tackle box
and wandered up the bank to study
a rotting grease spot on the sand,

one of dozens melting down   *Lord of the Flies.*
under a mat of slick black flies;
my mind awash with stink and buzzing,
I wondered how they'd surfaced there,   *"I will make you*
                                                Fishers of men."

until a fisherman below me raised his rod
in a sudden arc and brought in something
huge. "Another goddamn drum," he mumbled
as he tossed it up where I stood on the bank.

I watched the brilliant silver fish   *What's wrong with it?*
flop and gasp on the burning sand,   *It's beautiful.*
and all at once I understood.
I went back and sat with my uncle.
I thought of the fishers of men.

But, do some Christians
do ...

Did Jesus intend, in his
metaphor, that the bad
fish be culled? I think
the metaphor only went
as far as the act of
collecting. If you took it
too far — we'd eat what
was caught.

The River

Once more the western sky is turning red.
A few faint eastern stars begin to shine.
The river bleeds on, dark as oil through wood,
thin moonlight changing water into wine.
A great-horned owl dips silent as the sun;
a deer mouse pauses over its last meal,
looks heavenward too late to dodge or run.
The talons of winged mystery prevail.
A coyote's mournful hymn rings down the night,
far call to souls abandoned on this plane,
lost siren singing loneliness and fright,
forlorn as echoes of an orphan train.
The current pulls it all around the bend,
the only promise, water without end.

Neil Harrison

*In 1800, an estimated 60 million bison roamed
the North American continent. In 1889, by one
estimate, less than 1,100 remained.*[1]

Those Were the Days

We followed the rails
crossing Nebraska and Wyoming,
the devil's playground,
tracking the last of the buffalo,

And woke one August morning
to an ungodly roaring—
bulls at the wallow, rutting,
some three miles east the old man said.

We crossed ourselves, and laughing,
brought in the horses, hitching
them to the wagons, loading what
we'd need in the days ahead,

Then whipped the horses,
reining them toward a rough outcropping
between us and a massing darkness
wide as the plain beyond.

We left the horses blowing
as we climbed the rocks,
stalking low, into the sun
dawning blood-red in the billowing dust.

We saw the prairie
crawling with bison that dark morning,
and then we started shooting,
and watched them die all afternoon.

[1]from *Where Buffalo Roam*, Schult & Haugen, Badlands Natural History Association, Interior, SD 57750, 1979.

In Good Hands
(for Kathleen)

So they took him away,
the neighbor's little boy,
used to call across the street
when I worked on my car
"Hey mister, whatcha doin?"
that face always fathomless
as his question, effectively
curbing the curses, my habitual
soliloquy when under the hood.

They put him in some school,
skinny seven-year-old,
used to wander the neighborhood
stick in hand, staring
at the ground or searching
the sky, studying mysteries
out of reach of the rest of us,
in perpetual dialogue with his
invisible friend or foe.

It was best for him they said,
poor lamb lost in a wilderness,
a much safer place for him to be
with others of a similar nature,
little danger there of harming
himself or anyone's property,
insignificant leprechaun
touched at birth
but by what hand?

We curse on now without him,
secure again in our neighborhood
in the land of the fully insured,
where we're guaranteed numb
to that subtle touch in every heartbeat,

in the land of the fully insured,
where we're guaranteed numb
to that subtle touch in every heartbeat,
every breath, no matter how unfelt—
a gift, and no one,
no one knows the Giver.

Fighting the Night

Lights from the fishing camp
come off the black water
where we troll weedbeds after dark
under a Minnesota volley of stars,
stringing an occasional rock bass
red-eyed in the lantern light.

Going out I'd swear I could
walk on the water sliding under
the boat like a new-waxed floor,
but coming in I know I'd slip
through the surface and go down.

Gliding back and forth
trailing two-tailed twisters,
half asleep and sinking
into silent dreams,
knowing we must go on like this
as long as fish are biting.

Claude

Sprawled on the floor in front of the T.V.
he snores through sitcoms, nods off mid-way
into conversations, but mention hunting
and something wakes inside this man,
wilder than anything he's done in years;

suddenly more heart than swollen paunch,
he talks longbows and days gone by,
his face a muscled beast
gathering itself in the shadowed crags,
the broken dreams beneath his brows.

When his story ends, I stare in awe
of the predator crouched in this crippled form.
A narcoleptic man leans back on a sofa,
closes his eyes; a mysterious animal
slips silently back to the night.

Bison Bison

At the national refuge east of Valentine,
moving en masse in the morning mist, wild,
unpredictable, dangerous; stout backs
sloped like pathways to heaven, heads
bowed low, moaning prayers to the earth,
they've haunted my dreams for years.

The bull on the throne at the center
of the earth waits to light the pipe
full of killers of his kind; nostrils smoking,
eyes a red blaze, he counts the days
to judgment, silent, white, terrible.

A winter night at the livestock market,
I got a strange feeling and glanced
to my left, then up into the face
of an old brown bull towering over
the bars of a bed-frame stall.

His stare went through and far beyond me,
a ghost of something gone somewhere else,
back of the eyes of a stalled giant,
where misplaced gods haunt the morning mist,
wild, unpredictable, dangerous.

Those Miles
(for Arn)

On Merritt Reservoir I sat in the bow of his
fishing boat, my back to the wind, fingers
on the gunwales tingling under the cold spray
as he steered the boat west into the chop,

gazing up into the hills, barely a glance
at the water, until he cut the motor
far up the lake where the Snake comes in
and told me, "Sometime read OLD JULES."

He looked off again and spoke across the water,
"When I imagine this place before they dammed
the river, I can see him crawling those miles
alone through the hills with his shattered leg."

I glanced at the Sandhills beyond him
but didn't see it, him sitting in the stern,
staring across the water, the ragged pieces
of shrapnel in his leg forty years after the war.

Anchored in his secret spot, sitting on a school
of giant walleyes, he told me how they sometimes bite
so soft you need to wait to set the hook.
That afternoon I caught my first trophy fish.

Five summers later, a copy of OLD JULES on the seat
beside me, I drove across the Sandhills, headed west
to the Pine Ridge, south to the Niobrara, and came back
east through those hills alone in a red canoe.

And at the end of each day afloat on the river
I read until dark beside the Running Water,
and every night by the fire I saw him
crawling miles alone through the hills.

Prayer and Omen

Here is the place I told you of,
this high knob with the crooked pine,
sudden drop to the cottonwoods
and hidden trickle of Chadron Creek,
rattle of cicadas in the ponderosas
on this mile of ridge above Glen Road,

where doe and fawns flit, cautious
through the shadows, sensing a foreign
presence on the crest, our scent
like something black descending
with night to the valley and the meadow beyond,

the summer camp where day to day
kids stand in line at various stations,
waiting, hoping to encounter nature
through the mediation of counselors
in their insulated areas of expertise.

Now, all quiet on the dark meadow,
like a singular star in the August night
candlelight flickers on in a window,
a tentative glow on the eastern side,
desperate prayer or stubborn omen
in a world dying, still trying to be born.

Neil Harrison

Remembering the Wind Rivers
(for Larry)

Ancient as the fresh wet
scent of mountain earth,
raw as the odor of pack-string horses
steaming under rain-sopped pines,

that peculiar mix of aromas
rising from a damp campfire,
woodsmoke, grilled fish, and instant coffee
steeped in memory blurred by mist.

Watering the Horses

I walk to the tank in the autumn dusk
and listen to the weanling calves come in,
calling for their mothers, bawling for their lives;
the same sounds, same light
as twenty years ago on the Baylor place
two days after Margaret died on the highway.

Stock tank overflowing, John's mill whirring
in a chill north wind, we stopped to water the horses
as our string of calves moved up the trail.
I rubbed cold fingers and glanced at John,
grey as stone in the saddle on his black.

I couldn't find words for what I felt
and he held it all inside like tears.
We listened to the bawling calves,
to water spilling in and out of the tank.
A hawk screamed once, slipped south on the wind;
the horses seemed a long time drinking.

When they raised their heads and backed away,
we tightened our reins, headed them east,
and pushing a handful of stragglers
off the last green grass, we followed
the familiar cries into the hills.

Brothers

(for Dave)

We crossed the frozen channel in the dark,
set out decoys and huddled in the blind
over coffee and the Coleman stove,
hunting a last time together,
no mention of your separation,
not a word about impending divorce,
the young Lab shaking wild between us
as dawn flowered like blood on water,
drawing black lines of geese along the river.

They were high and stayed up, the day
clear and cold, but we hunkered until dark
on the frozen river, brothers
in a more natural sense than law,
shivering with the dog when the stove went out,
watching the sky and calling, calling
all that long day on the Platte,
waiting for something, a straggler, a loner,
for one last shot before the light ran out.

This Time

After the picnic in the park,
rod in hand, facing the river
you're standing ankle-deep in mud,
watching water climb the banks,
the current swelling with debris;

out of reach of a ready carcass,
without a maggot or a piece of meat,
you sever the tip of your little finger,
blood-baiting what you know is down there

breathing swirls of yellow dirt,
this fat world boiling fast away
its brush and trash and fallen trees,
posts and wire and bloated cattle,
abandoned buildings, habitations,

the twisted faces of the living and dead,
the vast earth coming clean once more,
but no ark waiting in the wings this time,
and no one left wild enough to walk on water.

Bringing the Arrowed Fish In

I've missed seven shots,
but I finally connect on a large male
and wind the heavy line onto the bow-reel
as fast as my wrist will rotate
bringing the arrowed fish in.

When he's close I grasp
the long shaft quivering in his side,
then force his slippery head down into the mud
where I can get a grip on it.

Pushing the metal point of the stringer
into the hollow behind the hard lips,
I pull the nylon cord through,
and slide the carp out of the water
where I can work the arrow back
through the hole in its side.

Knee-deep in black muck in the shallow bog
we call Spring Lakes, I watch carp
working the rushes to either side of me,
dark backs emerging through the glare
on the water, bellies ploughing
furrows in the soft mud.

My uncle grins from the car on the road
as I slog back through the deep sludge
with one of the fish I will give him
when I take him home, wishing
I had more to offer, recalling
the gunny sacks he filled with carp
the spring he picked me up from school,

the first time I saw carp spawning,
so thick he'd spear them two at a time,
shake them off in the grass behind,

and thrust again—a tall man
with a long spear in a world of fish
for the taking; young and wild
and full of life, with a quick temper,
a growing family and a penchant
for cards and booze.

Now, nearly blind and unable to stand
on even solid ground for long, my uncle
watches me bring in the last fish,
one of three I will offer him, shot low
in the belly, like the others we see
when we lay them side by side.
I've been aiming too fast, shooting too low.

And So

It ends one fine spring day; you kneel
in a field of brome, hands full of clay.

You walk once more to the river and stay
to wash what you can of those years away.

Hunting the High Plains
(for Larry Holland, 1937-1999)

Two steps behind him
on a ten-inch-wide trail
across the face of a sandstone bluff
three hundred feet above the Niobrara,

I watch as he eases into a crouch
and onto one knee, slowly
raising his rifle, aiming down
toward the base of the cliff

where I glimpse the four-point
over his shoulder, fat whitetail
with a swollen neck, head down,
following his nose.

Trailing does across the river,
the buck steps off the bank
into the open water.

I know this man,
and this animal is dead
even as the gentle wash of its wading
merges with the murmur of the Running Water.

I know this man,
and in the singular peace
at the heart of this timeless panorama
he's found what he was hunting.

Coming Off the Island This November Evening
(for Bill Kloefkorn)

At dusk I shoulder my rifle,
and splash through the rippled shallows
into the north channel of the Platte
a quarter mile down from where it
ran waist-high this morning.

Angling toward a slash of moonlight,
a beaver-slide off the dark north bank,
I pause midstream as the water piles up,
pinning the waders to my breast,
and I'm half afloat, probing the bottom,

when the sand beneath my right boot crumbles
and I'm one more piece of flotsam on the Platte,
riding a gentle current east, my feet
blunt stumps suspended in the waders,
reaching down, searching, as the white slide,
the dark willows slowly slip away.

The water holds an inch below
the lip of brown rubber, until I drift in
close enough I can get a bite on the bottom,
then wade up shallow near the bank,
and work upstream to the slide.

On the moon-white sand in the beaver run
I lie staring at the stars, the air so damp,
so rich with the scent and murmur of moving water,
even the common violence of traffic on the interstate
can't penetrate my sense of peace,
of oneness with this river.

Grateful acknowledgment is made to the editors of these publications:

"The Picture in My Hand" appeared in slightly different form in Nebraska Poets Calendar, Black Star Press, P.O. Box 6165, Lincoln, NE 68506, 2000.

"Hunting the High Plains" and "Remembering the Wind Rivers" appeared in slightly different form in The Plain Sense of Things, 3: A Tribute to Larry Holland. Sandhills Press, c/o Mark Sanders, College of the Mainland, 1200 Amburn Rd., Texas City, TX 77591, 1999.

"The Last Day of October" appeared in Nebraska Poets Calendar, Black Star Press, P.O. Box 6165, Lincoln, NE 68506, 1999.

"October" appeared in Yarrow, Dept. of English, Kutztown University, Kutztown, PA 19530, Fall/Winter, 1997.

"Prayer and Omen" appeared in WORDART, The Lakeland Center for Creative Arts, Arts on the Park, Inc., 115 N. Kentucky Ave., Lakeland, FL 33801, February, 1997.

"The Sandhills Night," "Story," "Remembering Sand," "The Last Day of October," "At Blue Hole," and "Hunting the Cool of the Day" appeared in The Plain Sense of Things: Eight Poets from Outstate Nebraska. Sandhills Press, c/o Mark Sanders, Humanities Team, College of the Mainland, 1200 Amburn Rd., Texas City, TX 77591, 1997.

"Brothers" appeared in Flyway, Iowa State University, Ames, IA, Winter, 1997, vol. 3:3.

"Autumn" appeared in Nebraska Poet's Calendar, Black Star Press, P.O. Box 6165, Lincoln, NE 68506, 1996.

"Before We Fell," "Perspective," "Familiar," "Flush!" "Fighting the Night," "Claude," "Bringing the Arrowed Fish In," "Sunrise on the Verdigris," "Some Nights," and "Pterodactyls" appeared in Story [a chapbook of poems], Logan House Press, Route 1, Box 154, Winside, NE 68790, 1995.

"Flood" appeared in Yarrow, Fall/Winter, 1993.

"Watering the Horses" appeared in Writer's Forum, University of Colorado at Colorado Springs, University Press of Colorado, P.O. Box 849, Niwot, CO 60544, 1993.

"Flush" appeared in Yarrow, Dept. of English, Kutztown University, Kutztown, PA 19530, Fall/Winter 1990.

"Before We Fell" and "Some Nights" appeared in The Nebraska Review, Writer's Workshop, University of Nebraska at Omaha, Omaha, NE 68182-0324, Fall/Winter 1989.

"Bringing the Arrowed Fish In" appeared in Yarrow, Dept. of English, Kutztown University, Kutztown, PA 19530, Fall/Winter 1989.

"Hunting the Cool of the Day" appeared in Poetry of Nebraska, Nebraska English Journal, Kearney State College, Kearney, NE 68849, Fall/Winter 1989.

Neil Harrison received a Bachelor of Arts degree in English and Biology from Chadron State College, a Master's degree in English from the University of Nebraska at Lincoln, and is currently completing an MFA in Creative Writing at Vermont College.

He has held interim and part-time teaching positions at Wayne State College since 1990 and at Northeast Community College since 1987. He grew up in Norfolk, Nebraska, and developed an early love for the Nebraska outdoors that has taken him across the state, from the northeast to the Sandhills, the Platte Valley, the Salt Valley, and the Pine Ridge.

His creative work has appeared in *The Nebraska Poets Calendar, The Plain Sense of Things, Yarrow, WordArt, Onionskin, Flyway, Writer's Forum, Story, Here from There, The Nebraska Review, The Nebraska English Journal, Nebraska Territory, The Platte Valley Review,* and others.